M000041135

The
CROSS—
the
Touchstone
of Faith

JESSIE PENN-LEWIS

CHRISTIAN · LITERATURE · CRUSADE
FORT WASHINGTON, PA 19034

CHRISTIAN LITERATURE CRUSADE

U.S.A.
P.O. Box 1449, Fort Washington, PA 19034

GREAT BRITAIN
51 The Dean, Alresford, Hants., SO24 9BJ

AUSTRALIA
P.O. Box 91, Pennant Hills, N.S.W. 2120

NEW ZEALAND
10 MacArthur Street, Feilding

Originally published by
The Overcomer Literature Trust
England

This Revised American Edition 1995

ISBN 0-87508-730-2

CONTENTS

JESSIE Penn-Lewis's scriptural sources included the Authorized, or King James, Version (A.V.), the English Revised Version of 1881 (R.V.), and the Conybeare and Howson translation of Paul's Epistles (C.H.). Unless otherwise indicated, Mrs. Penn-Lewis quoted the Authorized Version. Also she used Dr. C.I. Scofield's notes in his King James Version.

The
CROSS—
the
Touchstone
of Faith

JESSIE PENN-LEWIS

CHAPTER 1

THE BLOOD OF HIS CROSS

*"The Church of God, which He pur-
chased with His own blood"*
(Acts 20:28)

ONE of the scarcely realized results of
the thought currents moving in the
world today is the effect they are having
upon the professing Church of Christ—for
the most part unknown to itself—and even
upon many in the church who are true
believers in the gospel of Calvary.

The Apostle Paul speaks of "*winds* of doctrine," thus indicating that there are aerial
movements of doctrinal thought which
have an effect upon souls caught by them,
as though they were children carried by a
nurse—*any* nurse (Gr.)! "Children, tossed
to and fro, and blown round by every shift-
ing current of teaching" is Conybeare's ren-
dering of Ephesians 4:14. The word translated "wind" in the A.V. refers to air in mo-

tion, or a stream of air. How few preachers and teachers today realize the existence of such a "stream," and the danger of being caught in it. Many think they have arrived at the doctrine they hold by careful deliberation and study, oblivious of the revelation-fact that the "prince of the power of the air," who originates and governs these aerial movements of thought, blinds the minds of the unbelieving, while allowing his victims to think they are free men.

It is easy to recognize the Satanic source of these doctrinal thought-currents by words which are objected to, or dropped out of use, as "out-of-date for the people of today." One primary key word is the *blood* of Christ in connection with the way of salvation.

For some years there has been a growing shrinking from the use of this word, until there is almost open revolt at present among those who desire to be up-to-date preachers. And on the part of some who know the gospel truth, there is a silence on the theme without deliberate purpose or any suspicion of the influence of "modern thought" (satanic "air-currents") upon the mind. Today the stream of modern thought as "air-currents" is running strong, and it takes clear vision and a divine enduement of power to withstand its pressure.

The question is, <u>Can we eliminate, or</u> <u>even minimize the message of the gospel,</u> <u>as set forth in the language of the Bible on</u> <u>the sacred theme of the blood of the cross,</u> <u>without co-working with the prince of the</u> <u>power of the air, and causing the eternal</u> <u>ruin of multitudes of human beings</u>? Is there a "gospel" apart from the blood of the cross, or a true statement of the gospel possible with the message of the blood omitted? Can preachers of the gospel yield to the doctrinal air-currents of today and substitute the word "life" (the blood is the life) for the word "blood" without compromising with the "spirit of the age" and "bowing down to Baal"—its Prince?

With these questions in mind, let us go to the Word of God and ponder the story of Calvary. We will turn first to John 19:33 and 34, and reverently read the words of the apostle as he describes what he saw as he stood by the cross of the Lord Jesus. We are told that when the soldiers found Him dead, one of them with a spear pierced His side, and there came out "blood and water." It is noteworthy that although John had seen many marvelous miracles wrought by the God-Man before His death, it is not until he saw this exceptional sight that he is moved to exclaim in astonishment and awe, "He that saw it *bare record*," and "he *knoweth* that he saith true" (v. 35). What was it that was so astonishing in what had occurred that John departs from his usual self-effacement in recording the mighty works of Christ to affirm and reaffirm the truth of his words?

What did the apostle see? *Blood and water breaking out from the side of a dead man.* Was this "natural" or was it one of the miracles of the passion and death of the God-Man which lift His death altogether out of the realm of the ordinary, showing that He died neither as a "martyr" nor an "example," but as God Incarnate expiating the sin of a fallen race and providing out of His own outpoured blood a "fountain" for the cleansing of the guilt and power of the sins of millions of sinful human beings?

But let us go back a little in the sacred story, and see how marvelous was the redemptive work of the God-Man in the "shedding of blood" for the remission of sins, and how it was only possible by the power of the Eternal Spirit for Him as "very man of very man" thus to offer Himself without spot to God. Reading the type in Leviticus in the light of the antitype of the Gospels, how true were the words written of the High Priest, "He shall *flay* the burnt offering" (Leviticus 1:6). And how marvelous the pen portrait of Isaiah when he wrote, 400 years before the Lamb of Calvary died at Golgotha, that He was "wounded," "bruised," "stricken," and *His visage and His form so marred* from "the form of man . . . that His appearance was not that of a son of man."*

Let us now trace the stages of the expiatory sacrifice of God's provided Lamb, and see how full and entire was the shedding of blood for the remission of the sins of the world. First there was:

1. THE SWEAT OF BLOOD in Gethsemane (Luke 22:44). Luke, who was a physician, alone records this part of the anguish in Gethsemane. The God-Man could "feel the fatal distension of the heart, the coldness of the extremities, the difficult breathing," as "great drops of bloody perspiration fell to the ground"—all indicating "near rupture of the heart caused by mental agony." But He must not die in Gethsemane. With His heart at the point of rupture He cried to the Father (Hebrews 5:7), and "there appeared unto Him an angel strengthening Him" (Luke 22:43), and by the power of the Eternal Spirit, God Incarnate in the flesh went forward in the path of the blood shedding.

---

* Isa. 52:14, Scofield's note.

2. THE SCOURGING in the Hall of Pilate (Matthew 27:26). Here the leathern thongs of the scourge, each armed with an angular bony hook or sharp-sided cube, cut deeper and deeper into His sacred form, penetrating almost to the marrow, until His whole back appears an enormous wound. And then:

3. THE CROWN OF THORNS (Matthew 27:29–30) is placed upon His brow, and beaten down upon the head, until the veins give forth the sacred stream, and His visage is marred so that His appearance is not as a son of man. Then it is written, "They crucified Him," and we read of:

4. HIS PIERCED HANDS AND FEET (Luke 23:33; John 20:25), out of which broke forth again the outpoured blood, every part of His body having given forth the sacrificial stream in fulfillment of the type, "[the priest] shall *flay* the burnt offering" (Leviticus 1:6).

A Christian physician points out in connection with this marvelous record of physical suffering—sufficient in one phase alone, that of Gethsemane, to end the life of the strongest man—how the Godhead of Him who was God Incarnate in human guise shone out again and again in manifestation of Deity. For example:

(a) The "I am" of Jehovah-Jesus when the

mob that came to take Him "went backward and fell to the ground" (John 18:6), until He voluntarily permitted them to bind Him and lead Him away.

(b) The physical miracle on the cross when, at the sixth hour of His hanging there, He cried with a loud voice (Matthew 27:46)—for after great loss of blood, with tongue, mouth, and throat dried (Psalm 22:15; Psalm 69:3) it is usually impossible to articulate words.

(c) The majesty and full consciousness of Deity when He deliberately bowed His head and "dismissed His spirit" (Matthew 27:50, lit. Greek, Scofield) with the cry, "Accomplished."

The rupture of the heart was at last allowed to take its course. It had been, we may reverently say, held back until the blood-shedding was carried out to the full. "It is the *blood* that maketh atonement for the soul" (Leviticus 17:11). It had now been poured out to the uttermost in the midst of shame (Psalm 69:7) and horror (Psalm 55:5) unparalleled, but with outshinings of Deity which made the path of unspeakable shame aglow with the glory of a conqueror.

Here we reach the point of the miracle, the very recording of which awakens the apostle's outburst of emphatic declaration of what he *saw* and *affirmed* as *true. What* did he see?

The expiatory blood-shedding was over. The Victim-Victor hung lifeless on the tree, when to John's amazement, as the soldier's spear struck deep into the heart, there came forth blood and water. A Christian physician writes concerning this miracle, "Some think the 'water' was fluid from the pericardium (the serous covering around the heart), but this fluid is very small in quantity, and is of a different consistency and character to water. Others say it was serum derived from the blood, but serum only becomes separated from the blood when it is clotting. The *Scripture* says 'blood and water,' not clot and serum. . . ." There was also another thing that John saw, the wonderment of which only physicians would recognize. "In a human body," writes the aforesaid Christian physician, "if a clean-cut wound, as with a sharp double-edged spear, be made *before* death, there occurs immediately a gaping wound. The living muscles being always on the stretch, as soon as they are severed they retract and leave an open space. *But a wound made in a body after death leaves no gaping wound.* The muscular fibers being dead are inelastic and do not retract. . . ." Yet the Lord said to Thomas after He was risen again, "Reach hither thy hand and put it into My side; and be not faithless, but believing . . ." (see John 20:20, 25, 27–28, R.V.).

"Blood and water" from the pierced side. Have we not here the *fountain opened* of which the deepest-taught saints have sung, and into which the deepest-dyed sinners have plunged in myriads, since the Tragedy-Victory of Golgotha? How can this message ever be translated into "modern terms" with the same meaning, and with the certainty of the same witness of the Holy Spirit which causes the one who believes in the efficacy of that blood to *know* that there is nothing between him and a Holy God?

No, it remains true:

> "There is a fountain filled with blood
>   Drawn from Immanuel's veins,
> And sinners plunged beneath that flood
>   Lose all their guilty stains."

Since the outshinings of Deity accompanied the tragic death of God Incarnate in flesh as the propitiation for the sins of the whole world (1 John 2:2), the *language* conveying the message of the expiatory death must be understood as it is used in *heaven* by those who see Calvary as God sees it, and not according to the carnal mind of the fallen creation.

"I beheld, and lo a great multitude . . . clothed with white robes. . . . And one said . . . What are these . . . and whence came they? And I said unto him, Sir, thou knowest. And he said, These are they which . . . have washed their robes, and made them white in the blood of the Lamb . . ." (Revelation 7:9–14).

The out-poured blood of the Son of God is here described as a "fountain" into which myriads of sin-stained spirits have plunged and been made clean. The "water" which accompanied the blood, out of the "riven side" of the Lamb of God, in the language of heaven depicts the "river of water of life . . . proceeding out of the throne of God and of the Lamb" (Revelation 22:1). For the cross on Golgotha was that throne on *earth*, when God Incarnate hung upon it, and the throne in heaven has in its midst, for all eternity, a "Lamb as it had been slain" (Revelation 5:6).

But the expiatory death on Calvary meant more than propitiation for the sins of the world. It had a *representative* meaning which Christ Himself revealed to the Apostle Paul, after He had ascended to glory. The gospel which Paul preached was not the result of his Jewish upbringing, as may be seen by the fact that the bitterest opponents to his message were his Jewish compatriots.

The gospel of the "blood" was a revelation-fact made known to Paul by the very One who had shed His blood at Golgotha. It was He, too, who revealed to Paul (Galatians 1:11–12) that in all He had gone through, He had suffered as the representative of the fallen race, "*made sin*" to suffer to the depths the penalty of sin. And even more, *identified with the sinner,* to carry to the cross the sinner as well as his sins. (See Romans 6:1–14.)

While, therefore, we sing with grateful hearts, "Blessed be the fountain of blood, to a world of sinners revealed," and recognize that we need perpetually to remain under the power of that cleansing stream, let us remember also that the sacred fountain of blood was not opened merely to cleanse or to shelter the fallen creation.

Here comes in the message of the Apostle Paul, repeated by him again and again. The God-Man died upon a cross. He shed His blood in expiation for sin, but also as the One identified with the sinner for whom He died—so the sinner *himself* died on that cross *identified* with his Substitute. Therefore the apostle reiterates "*Ye died*" (Colossians 3:3), "*all died*" (2 Corinthians 5:14), "we who *died*" (Romans 6:2), "now having *died*" (Romans 7:6). "They that are

Christ's *have crucified the flesh*" (Galatians 5:24), and having died with their Savior, pass with Him into a new world to walk in newness of life.

The "blood and water," therefore, which the awestruck Apostle John saw as he stood by the cross of Jesus, has a two-fold meaning of death and life for all for whom He died: death with the One who died on the cross, and the inflow of the "water of life" in life-giving power so that out of the redeemed one should flow rivers of living water.

THE PRECIOUS BLOOD OF CHRIST

(1) THE OUTPOURED BLOOD
1. As Propitiation   Romans 3:25
2. As Redemption   1 Peter 1:18-19; Ephesians 1:7
3. As a "purchase" price   Acts 20:28
4. As the ground of peace   Colossians 1:20
5. As the ground of "justification"—
   i.e., the sinner declared guiltless   Romans 5:9

(2) THE BLOOD WITHIN THE VEIL
1. He entered through the blood   Hebrews 9:12
   (*See Hebrews 9:7, 9:25*)
2. Believers have access by the blood
                           Hebrews 10:19
3. Believers are "made nigh by the blood
   of Christ"   Ephesians 2:13

(3) THE BLOOD APPLIED TO THE BELIEVER
  1. The type of "sprinkling" for remission of
     sin   Hebrews 9:18–23
       (*See also Hebrews 12:22–24*)
  2. The blood to the conscience   Hebrews 9:14
       (*See also Hebrews 10:22*)
  3. The blood "sanctifying" or setting apart for
     God   Hebrews 13:12
  4. The blood of the covenant the ground of God's
     work in the soul   Hebrews 13:20–21
  5. ". . . Loosed us from our sins in His blood . . ."
                              Revelation 1:5 (R.V., mg.)

(4) THE CONDITION FOR THE PERPETUAL APPLI-
    CATION OF THE BLOOD
       "If we walk in the light, as He is in the light,
    we have fellowship one with another, and the
    blood of Jesus, His Son, cleanseth us from all
    sin."   1 John 1:7

(5) THE BLOOD OF THE LAMB SHED AND APPLIED
    BY THE SPIRIT OF GOD, THE WEAPON OF VIC-
    TORY OVER SATAN
       "They overcame him by the blood of the Lamb
    and by the word of their testimony; and they
    loved not their lives unto the death."
                                    Revelation 12:11

"Precious blood, by this we conquer
      In the fiercest fight:
Sin and Satan overcoming
      By its might."

(*Hymns of Consecration and Faith*)

CHAPTER 2

THE "CROSS" AND THE "BLOOD"

WHAT IS THE DIFFERENCE?

A N evangelist, seeking to know the full meaning of Galatians 2:20, writes as follows:

I think I have a deeper insight into what the cross of Christ means with regard to victory. One morning I awoke with sickening dread and terror upon me. I pleaded with the Lord to show me how to get deliverance, for I knew that such fear was sin. I prayed: "Holy Spirit, bury me deep in the death of Christ, and apply the full power of the blood." It seemed almost like repeating a "charm," until I said: "Apply the full power of the victory won over Satan and his host at Calvary, and deliver me . . . !" Five minutes later I was singing, "Praise God from whom all blessings flow."

As we read this we ask: What was the difference between asking for the "full power of the blood," and the "full power of the victory won over Satan and his host at Calvary"? The theological question we will not touch. Our purpose is simply to record experiential provings of the Word, so that we may know what "works" in actual life-reality in these days of peril.

This distinction between asking for (1) the power of the blood and (2) the effect of the victory of Calvary has come to our notice from several directions.

A brother in Christ, to whom the above letter was shown, said that he had found exactly the same difference, although he had worked it in another manner. In conflict or temptation, he had claimed the "blood," but the victory did not come until he cried: "ALL THAT CALVARY MEANS." Appropriating that as the weapon, there was instant deliverance. Another worker was in a meeting where satanic powers were most manifestly at work. He sat still and quietly "claimed the victory of Calvary" over all hell, and as he maintained that attitude and stayed *there—at Calvary*—the meeting was released from the power of the adversary.

(1) THE VICTORY OF THE CROSS

It was the appeal to the *victory* aspect of Christ's work at Calvary which brought the witness of the Holy Spirit, proving that the "prince of this world hath been judged" (John 16:11, R.V.)—yes, conquered at Calvary. This shows that in these days of severe conflict with the powers of darkness, we must cease to theorize on the subject and take what the Spirit of God desires to teach us by these provings of spiritual things and seek intelligently to understand their meaning.

There are many aspects of the finished work of Christ on the cross of Calvary, and each meets a special need in the experiential deliverance of the sinner. For instance, when a soul needs the message of Calvary for reconciliation with God, we do not point him to conformity to Christ's death—but we seek to show him the aspect which meets his condition, and the Holy Spirit then bears witness to the truth in instant power.

(2) VARIOUS ASPECTS OF THE CROSS

In the same way, there are various aspects of the cross which meet the Christian's need, and the difference between claiming the "power of the blood" and "all that Calvary means" needs to be clearly defined. God would not have us hold a superstitious belief in the efficacy of the word "blood" as do darkened souls in the sign of the cross. We must understand *when* the truth about the blood of Christ is the right aspect of Calvary's work to lay hold of by faith, and when the "victory of the cross" meets the need. Neither must we forget that mere words about the sacred blood of the Lamb will no more avail than do words about the cross—unless behind the words is a direct cry to God Himself and the "power of the blood" is the particular aspect of the finished work of Christ which meets the need. Let us make it very clear that

(3) THE "BLOOD" DOES NOT CLEANSE THE "FLESH"

The subject of the precious blood and all that it means is too great to go into extensively here, but briefly, (1) the blood of Christ is spoken of in *relation to sin*; (2) the cross relates to the *crucifixion of the sinner* with the Savior (Galatians 2:20, 5:24, 6:14); and (3) *victory over Satan* comes through the death on Calvary (Hebrews 2:14). All passages of Scripture about the blood and the cross show this, and make it clear why we need to claim *both* to obtain victory. The power of the blood does not deal with the "flesh," which is Satan's "workshop," but with *sin*, according to 1 John 1:7. The "flesh" or old Adam life cannot be *cleansed*—it must be crucified. The blood is the poured-forth life of the Son of God as an expiatory sacrifice for *sin*. The *cross* speaks of the place where He was crucified, as the representative of the fallen race of Adam.

The context of the words, "They overcame him by the blood of the Lamb" (Revelation 12:11), shows that this is said of the *overcomers* who are in conflict with Satan as an accuser. These overcomers are described as those who "love not their lives *even unto death*," i.e., who LIVE and ACT in the spirit of the cross, and they cannot do this unless they first know the identification message of the cross in death to sin, and to the fallen life of the first Adam.

The overcomers are those who know the cross, and have "crucified the flesh" (Galatians 5:24); who have seen their death, on the cross with Christ, to the *world* (Galatians 6:14); who can give the word of their testimony to His finished work of redemption and victory, and are purposed to follow Him to Calvary and to love not their lives to the death.

(4) THE NORMAL POSITION OF THE BELIEVER

All truth would fall into right relationship to other truth if it were clearly understood that the cross is the focal point from which all truth radiates, and that the normal POSITION of every believer is, according to God's view and purpose, "crucified with Christ" (see Romans 6:3, 6).

A careful reading of all the Epistles of Paul will show that they are written on the basis of the cross set forth in Romans 6— the fact that God consigns the old fallen Adam to the cross, and has nothing to say to him.

God deals with all believers on this ground: "IN CHRIST YOU DIED." But the Church of Christ, as a whole, ignores this fact. It treats the fallen creation as capable of improvement, and the meaning of the cross—*bringing to death the old Adam race*, as fallen beyond repair—is thus nullified. Let us note yet again that

(5) THE "BLOOD" DOES NOT SHELTER THE "FLESH"

How we need to see this plainly, for we find that in all those who do not thus apprehend the truth of Christ's death on the cross in its manward aspect, the old Adam life is busy *appropriating truths which belong to the new creature* in Christ Jesus; hence the confusion of "views" and strange mixture of truth and error held by various sections of the professing Church. This is

especially serious when it comes to conflict with satanic powers, and when the
children of God ignorantly claim "the shelter of the blood" UPON THE UNCRUCIFIED
"FLESH"! For without the experiential knowledge of the crucifying power of the cross,
and an active moment-by-moment faith
that it is now crucified and out of action,
the "flesh" is not dealt with, but *remains
actively existent and open to the workings
of the spirits of evil*, even while the believer
is claiming the "shelter of the blood."

It cannot be said too strongly that the
precious blood of Christ was NOT MEANT TO
"SHELTER" THE UNCRUCIFIED "FLESH" any
more than it was intended as a cloak to
sin. God does not promise to shield or de-
fend by the blood of His Son what He has
condemned to death in the death of His
Son. It is not belittling the efficacy of the
sacred blood to say it does not do more or
less than "according to the Scriptures." To
speak, therefore, of the blood cleansing the
heart from sin and not to understand, as
correlative truth, the believer "crucified
together with Christ," is failing to apprehend the full power of the work of redemption at Calvary.

(6) WHEN THE "BLOOD" CLEANSES

The blood continuously cleansing ac-

cording to 1 John 1:7 is ONLY FOR THE BE-
LIEVER WHO "WALKS IN THE LIGHT AS GOD IS IN
THE LIGHT." For this he must be steadily
abiding on the foundation fact of his death
with Christ. Then, and only then, can he
walk in the blaze of divine light and find
the blood of Jesus Christ, God's Son, being continuously applied for the "cleansing from all SIN."

(7) DEATH IDENTIFICATION WITH CHRIST

The sixth chapter of Romans presents
not an *aspect* of truth, but the FOUNDATION
TRUTH upon which every believer must
stand to know anything about victory. It
not only reveals the very heart of Calvary,
but the very heart of the resurrection. Calvary means the death-identification of the
believer with Christ, so that he lives and
moves in a spiritual sphere in resurrection
life. "Christ being raised from the dead
dieth no more; *death hath no more domin-
ion over him.* For in that He died, He died
unto sin once: but in that He liveth, He
liveth unto God. LIKEWISE RECKON YE also . . ."
writes the apostle to the Romans (6:9–11).

But we need to see too that there is a life
side to the sixth chapter of Romans, the
resurrection side. On the resurrection side
of the cross, "death" has no more domin-

ion. The negative side of "death" should not be dwelt upon to the exclusion of the positive LIFE SIDE of union with Christ. The death is to be reckoned an accomplished fact, every moment. But "Christ being raised, dieth no more." He is ALIVE, and the believer identified by faith with Him in death is united to Him in His life on the life side of the cross.

(8) HOW TO "RECKON" ON THE FACT OF THE CROSS

The believer must reckon that he HAS died—not that he is *going* to die. If he again and again asks God to "put to death" some one point, he will never realize the positive life power. Perhaps you are saying, "I have not 'died' to this and that." Take your position now on Romans 6:6, and then "reckon" yourself "ALIVE UNTO GOD"; and as you are alive unto God, you will surely come into conflict with the spiritual foes in the spiritual sphere, described in Ephesians 6:10–18. And standing on the foundation fact of Romans 6, you will go on to victory.

(9) THE HOLY SPIRIT'S WITNESS TO CALVARY

We have said the Holy Spirit bears instant witness to the aspect of Calvary which meets our need. The need of the writer of the letter quoted was "victory over Satan" because it was an attack of the *adversary* upon her. She required, of course, first the cleansing power of the blood from *sin*, but also the victory of the cross over Satan. In the case of the worker in the meeting, it was not the power of the blood, i.e., *cleansing*, which was needed, but the victory of Calvary over *Satan*. It was the evil spirits of Satan who were working upon the believers present, who knew nothing of the *message of the cross* in the aspect of crucifixion with Christ.

"ALL THAT CALVARY MEANS"

therefore embodies:

1. The *cross* as the basis upon which the believer stands, reckoning himself "dead indeed unto sin," and he himself alive unto God.

2. The *blood* of Jesus Christ continuously cleansing from every sin—from the Godward aspect—for the maintenance of undimmed fellowship with God, and with all who are joined to Christ.

3. The *victory* of the Lord upon the cross, over Satan, as the AGGRESSIVE WEAPON OF VICTORY over all the hosts of evil.

To recapitulate, we say again that the truth of Romans 6 and Galatians 2:20 concerns the personal *position* of the believer; the blood cleansing of 1 John 1:7 has to do with *sin* on the Godward side; and Revelation 12:11 deals with Satan as a personal *accuser*. Standing by faith on these statements of divine facts, the believer is then in a position to take aggressive action against the powers of darkness, with his weapon being the victory of the cross.

The following extract from a letter is a word in season from one who was shown by the Spirit of God the Romans 6 message of Calvary.

Christ made plainer to me than ever before the objective reality, literalness, sufficiency, completeness, and finality of my crucifixion with and in Christ on Calvary. I am believing that the objective phase, or better, FACT of the complete and finished death of my old man on the cross, as completed nineteen centuries ago in Christ when He said, "It is finished," is FAR GREATER IN ITS IMPORTANCE AND POTENCY than the subjective phase of my belief in this.

It is so, praise God, whether I believe it or not. Faith, I am seeing, is more common sense than anything else. FAITH IS JUST A RECOGNITION OF FACTS. And it is not hard to believe *facts* when you look them squarely in the face. A full view of the cross, and what was done there, makes faith easy.

May every reader of these words look the FACTS of Romans 6 full in the face and believe God. Then, go on in union with the living Christ to prove the way of victory over sin and Satan. Amen.

THE CROSS OF CALVARY

(1) THE PLACE OF THE SIN-BEARING BY THE SUBSTITUTE
1. He "bare our sins . . . on the tree, that we, being *dead* to sins, should live unto righteousness" 1 Peter 2:24
2. The Place of Reconciliation: "Reconciled by His *death* . . ." Romans 5:10

(2) THE PLACE OF THE "SINNER" CRUCIFIED
1. Our "old man crucified with Him . . . that henceforth . . . not serve sin" Romans 6:6
2. "I . . . crucified with Christ . . . not I but Christ liveth in me . . ." Galatians 2:20
3. "They that are Christ's have crucified the flesh" Galatians 5:24
4. "The world . . . crucified unto me . . ." Galatians 6:14

(3) THE PLACE OF UNITY BETWEEN BELIEVERS
"Reconcile both . . . by the cross, having slain the enmity thereby . . ." Ephesians 2:16

(4) THE PLACE OF THE OVERTHROW OF SATAN
"Principalities and powers, He made a show of . . . triumphing over them . . ." (i.e, through the cross) Colossians 2:15
(*See John 12:31; 16:11*)

(5) THE DEATH OF THE CROSS APPLIED TO THE
BELIEVER

"We who *died* . . ." Romans 6:2 (R.V.)

"Discharged . . . *having died*" Romans 7:6 (R.V.)

"Ye *died* with Christ . . ." Colossians 2:20 (R.V.)

"For *ye died* . . ." Colossians 3:3, 5 (R.V., mg.)

"For *if we died* with Him, we shall also live. . ."
2 Timothy 2:11 (R.V.)

(6) THE DEATH OF THE "SUBSTITUTE" THE DEATH
OF THE SINNER

"One died for all, therefore all *died*"
2 Corinthians 5:14 (R.V.)

(7) THE CONTINUITY OF THE "CROSS" FOR EVERY
BELIEVER AS WELL AS THE CONTINUAL APPLI-
CATION OF THE BLOOD

"Always delivered unto *death* . . . that the life
also of Jesus might be made manifest in our mortal flesh. So then, death worketh in us, but LIFE
in *you* . . ." 2 Corinthians 4:10–12

CHAPTER 3

THE "SELF-LIFE" UNVEILED

"I know that in me, that is, in my flesh,
dwelleth no good thing"
(Romans 7:18, R.V.)

CONYBEARE tells us that by the word "flesh" St. Paul generally denotes that which is earthly in man as opposed to that which is spiritual, and "no better practical and popular equivalent for such 'flesh' is to be found than the familiar word 'self'" (Moule).

When Adam fell, he fell under the power of the flesh, of the life of earth, instead of being dominated as he was before by the Spirit and the life of God; therefore God said:

"My Spirit shall not rule [or abide] in man . . . in their going astray *they are flesh*" (Genesis 6:3, R.V., mg.).

It is most important for us to understand what are the characteristics of the self-life, and how impossible it is, when under its sway, to live a spiritual life and wield spiritual weapons in the service of God. It is useless exhorting the "flesh" to be "spiritual"—and yet the flesh seeking to live a "spiritual" life and calling itself "spiritual" is the reason for the discrepancy in so many Christian lives today. We get light in our minds, spiritual phrases on our tongues, call our "work" spiritual, while we ourselves live after the flesh in greater or lesser degree all the time.

Let us then take the Scripture and ask that the sword of the Spirit may pierce to the joint and marrow, dividing soul and spirit, so that we may know where we actually stand in the sight of God.

THE FLESH

Let us note first that in our natural birth, we are born after the flesh.

> "That which is born of the flesh is flesh" (John 3:6).

Therefore it cannot be anything else but "flesh," neither can the "flesh" be changed into spirit by effort, or culture, or prayer.

The flesh is antagonistic to the Holy Spirit.

> "The flesh lusteth against the Spirit, and the Spirit against the flesh; for these are contrary the one to the other" (Galatians 5:17, R.V.).

The main characteristics of the "flesh."

1. It is by its nature at enmity with God.
   "The mind of the flesh *is* enmity against God" (Romans 8:7, R.V.).
2. It cannot submit to God because it is contrary to Him.
   "It is not subject [Gr., not able to submit] to the law of God" (Romans 8:7).
3. It minds earthly things because it is of the earth.
   "They that are after the flesh do mind the things of the flesh" (Romans 8:5).
4. All its outcome ends in death.
   "The mind of the flesh is death" (Romans 8:6, R.V.).

The child of God may be "yet carnal."

"I, brethren, could not speak unto you as unto spiritual, but as unto carnal, as unto babes in Christ" (1 Corinthians 3:1).

"Having begun in the Spirit, do ye now make an end in the flesh?" (Galatians 3:3, mg.)

"Whereas there is among you envying, strife, and divisions, are ye not carnal?" (1 Corinthians 3:3-4) said Paul to the Corinthians, while in his letter to the Galatians he classes "variance, emulations, strife and such like" with the grossest manifestations of the flesh, showing the one source of all.

Moreover, how genuine children of God have mourned over rebellion they cannot help! They are conscious of a lack of submission: they know they mind the things of earth, and are most in their element among them. They know it, grieve over it, fight against it, yet they cannot change themselves. Some make resolutions, redouble every effort and try every plan they can think of to make themselves more "spiritual." They consecrate and reconsecrate themselves to God, yet apparently in vain. Some think that others more "spiritual" must have some special gift, while they continue to mourn over their own coldness of heart and lack of Christlikeness.

Rebellion, disobedience, earthliness, powerlessness, these are the characteristics of the life after the flesh, but there are still more subtle ones laid bare in the Word of God.

THE MORE SUBTLE WORKS OF THE FLESH

1. *Judging* after the flesh (i.e., judging according to the outward appearance).

"Ye judge after the flesh; I judge no man. And yet if I judge, my judgment is true" (John 8:15–16; compare Isaiah 11:3).

2. *Purposing* after the flesh.

"The things that I purpose, do I purpose according to the flesh, that with me there should be yea yea, and nay nay?" (2 Corinthians 1:17).

3. *Boasting* after the flesh.

"Many glory after [i.e., in the manner of] the flesh" (2 Corinthians 11:18).

4. *Hoping* to make a good impression in the flesh.

"Many . . . desire to make a fair show in the flesh . . . only that they may not be persecuted for the cross of Christ." (Galatians 6:12, R.V.).

5. *Fighting* for God after the flesh.

"We do not war according to the flesh . . . the weapons of our warfare are not of the flesh" (2 Corinthians 10:3–4, R.V.).

6. *Friendships* in the flesh.

"We henceforth know no man after the flesh" (2 Corinthians 5:16).

7. *Knowing* Christ after the flesh.

"Though we have known Christ after the flesh, yet now we know Him so no more" (2 Corinthians 5:16, R.V.).

As children of God we may have been delivered from the more gross manifestations of the flesh, and yet these subtle ones remain.

Let us look at the list and prove our own selves! The judging after the sight of the eyes, according to earthly ideas rather than from the standpoint of God! The changeability which characterizes so many in the Master's service; the broken promises and broken engagements so lightly thought of, instead of the steadfast faithfulness after the pattern of Him who changeth not. The glorying over visible results; the gauging of the work of the Spirit of God by the multitude of converts, and measuring everything by outward appearance; caring "how things look" to others rather than having a single eye toward God; valuing the applause of the Christian world while failing in hidden service, and in the things which are least. Fighting for God, and often against each other, instead of *with* God against the powers of darkness, and depending upon earthly methods of winning the world to Christ.

Yes, even our friendships—our *Christian* friendships—may be "in the flesh," for how little we know of deepened and purified affection, with God between us and our dearest! Our very knowledge of Christ may have been mental or *intellectual light.* We may know all about Him, hold clear views, and know well the letter of the written Word—but the Christ who is the Living Word, we may not really know.

It is written "the flesh profiteth nothing" (John 6:63). Though we speak like angels— nothing! Though we understand all mysteries—nothing! Though we have all knowledge and faith to move mountains—nothing! Though we give all our possessions away, even sacrificing our bodies to be burned, it all profits nothing unless these actions are from the source of the life of God in us—the Life of Him who is Love.

GOD'S WAY OF DELIVERANCE

God's way of deliverance is through the death of Christ.

> "One died for all, therefore all died . . . that they which live should no longer live unto themselves, but unto Him" (2 Corinthians 5:14–15, R.V.).

The deliverance from the life after the flesh is through the finished work of the

Redeemer upon Calvary's cross, and until our eyes are opened to see our death *with* Christ, as well as His death *for* us, we must remain "in the flesh," and walk "after the flesh" in some degree.

We have wondered why our Christian lives seem to be ceaseless, toilsome effort. The answer is, we have not clearly understood that the *life of earth can never grow into the spiritual*, and that the "flesh" can never be improved or changed, but must be *crucified*.

We have obtained the forgiveness of our sins as we have believed God's Word that "One died for all," and we shall obtain deliverance from the life after the flesh just so far as we see that the sinner himself was *crucified with the Savior*, for "all died in Him" (Conybeare).

It is the work of the Holy Spirit to apply the deliverance of the cross.

> "The flesh lusteth against the Spirit, and the Spirit against the flesh . . . they that are of Christ Jesus have crucified the flesh" (Galatians 5:17, 24, R.V.).

These verses show that the pardoned sinner is not left alone in this battle, for the Holy Spirit, whom He made to dwell in us when He gave us the gift of eternal life, yearns over us with jealous envy. The Spirit evermore seeks to *bring to the cross* the "flesh" against which He fights with strong desire.

In actual experience, when we have apprehended our deliverance through death with Christ, the "self-life" often appears more "alive" than ever! Just here God would have us stand firm upon His written Word. The increasing revelation proves the surrender to the cross to be real, because the Holy Spirit takes us at our word and reveals all that He has seen lying underneath—reveals it that it may be dealt with at the cross. Our part is to yield our wills, and take God's side against ourselves, while the Holy Spirit applies the death of Christ to all that is contrary to Him that it may really be true that we who are of Christ have crucified the flesh with all its desires.

The practical and continual attitude to the "self-life."

1. "Make not *provision* for the flesh, to fulfill the lusts [desires] thereof" (Romans 13:14).

    It is absolutely necessary that we *account* ourselves crucified, and do not take the flesh into consideration, or provide for its likes and dislikes.

2. "Use not your freedom for an *occasion*

to the flesh" (Galatians 5:13, R.V.).

It must be given no opportunity to speak, no quarter whatever, for one degree of yielding will strengthen its life.

3. "Have no confidence in the flesh" (Philippians 3:3).

We must not rely upon it in anything, nor allow ourselves to admit a thought that we can do this or that; let us be willing to be as fools rather than that the flesh shall gain any glory.

4. Hate "the garment spotted by the flesh" (Jude 23).

Let us seek that God may give us such a sight of the corruption of the self-hood that we shall dread it, and fear it most under its most beautiful aspect.

THE LIFE IN THE SPIRIT

"Ye are not in the flesh, but in the Spirit, if so be that the Spirit of God dwelleth in you" (Romans 8:9, R.V.).

Just so far as the Eternal Spirit has room in us, so far we are "in the Spirit." God's purpose is that the Spirit should possess us wholly, so that we may not only *live* by the Spirit, but walk each day step-by-step in the Spirit, not fulfilling the desires of the flesh (Galatians 5:25).

As we apprehended the deliverance of the cross and the Holy Spirit manifests in us the glorious liberty of the children of God, we shall now know in truth:

The Spirit-leading as a little child
               (Romans 8:14).
The Spirit-cry of "Father" to the Father's
      heart   (Romans 8:15).
The Spirit-witness of the child-position
               (Romans 8:16).
The Spirit-intercession in the will of God
               (Romans 8:26).

Now, unto Him that is able to do exceeding abundantly above all that we ask or think, according to the power that worketh in us, unto Him be the glory. Amen.

"BEING MADE CONFORMABLE . . ."

What is the difference between "*I have been crucified with Christ*" (standing on Romans 6:11) and putting some newly discovered sin to the cross (*making to die the doings of the body*)?

Colossians 3:3–10 is the *experiential* side of Romans 6:6–11 in regard to sin, as 2 Corinthians 4:10–12 is the experiential side in regard to the manifestation of the life of Jesus, and blessing to others.

By faith you "reckon" that you have died

with Christ, and as you thus "reckon," the Holy Spirit applies that death to you as you obey the ever-increasing light He throws on your life and actions. The "objective" and "subjective" must be kept in balance. If you take Romans 6 as *absolute in experience* as well as in judicial position, without other Scriptures to interpret and supplement it, you will be in danger of not calling sin SIN; and you will close the door of your mind to the Holy Spirit's light upon deeper knowledge of yourself and God. You will be shut up to the simple maintaining of a "position," with no open vista of deeper experiential knowledge of Calvary and what Galatians 2:20 means. You "*have been* crucified with Christ"—yes—but every part of your whole being must be made "conformable to His death"—this includes the "self-life" as well as "sin." This will take the whole of one's lifetime, and the work will not be completed *subjectively* until even the body of our humiliation is "conformed to the body of His glory" (Philippians 3:21, R.V.). In other words, the objective fact of "died with Christ" is complete, but the *subjective application* from center to circumference ends only with the final redemption of the body, when He shall come to be admired in all them that believe (2 Thessalonians 1:10).

Galatians 2:20 is *the outcome of the faith position* of Romans 6. We "reckon" God's fact, and then declare "I have been crucified," while in detail we are day by day *made conformable* in experience and obey Romans 6:13 in practice.

CHAPTER 4

THE CROSS AND OUR WEAKNESSES

"Himself took our infirmities . . ."
(Matthew 8:17)

"Of myself I will not glory, but in mine infirmities . . ." (2 Corinthians 12:5)

A QUESTION has been already put to the children of God—one which has moved many hearts—regarding the extent to which we all would voluntarily choose that the depths of the cross should be produced *in us* by the Spirit of God.

Let us suppose that the question, How deep shall it go? has been settled in our individual lives—with a real cry to God that the Holy Spirit shall cut so deep that we truly experience the "life hid with Christ in God" in the innermost elements of our being. There yet remains what the Scripture describes as "*our infirmities.*" Has the cross nothing to say regarding them?

Let us turn to the Word of God for light upon this very vital and practical aspect of the Christian's life. First consider the word translated "infirmity" in the Authorized Version (K.J.V.). In the Revised Version it is rendered several times as "weakness" or "weaknesses." The Greek is *astheneia*—the word having in it the primary thought of lack of strength, feebleness or physical weakness. In some cases, however, it includes the dispositional weakness which every human being has in one form or another in his *character.* The word never refers to *sin* or disobedience to the known will of God; and God does not deal with real "infirmity" as such. This can be seen in the difference between His treatment of Elijah when he fled from the threats of Jezebel (1 Kings 19:1–3) and of Saul when he disobeyed the commands of God in respect to Amalek (1 Samuel 15).

But what has the cross to do with these "infirmities" or "weaknesses"—our weaknesses of character such as timidity, cowardice, fear, self-consciousness, impulsiveness, shyness, etc.? These arise, so to speak, from the shape of our "make-up," and every human being has a distinct and separate individuality even while manifesting certain idiosyncrasies obtained from one's ancestry. Is it possible to have the traits of weakness we have inherited come under the power of the cross, as well as our physical weaknesses? Must one's inner life of union with Christ be hindered in its manifestation to others by these "infirmities," or can the power of the cross deal with these as well as with one's old Adam life?

Surely it can. What do the Scriptures say?

First let us look at

(1) THE CROSS AND SICKNESS

"He cast out the spirits with His word and healed all that were sick: that it might be fulfilled which was spoken by Esaias the prophet, saying, Himself took our infirmities [astheneia] *and bare our sicknesses* [nosos]*"* (Matthew 8:16–17).

It should be noted that the Greek word for sickness—*nosos*—is distinct from *astheneia*—infirmity. The lexicon gives *nosos* as meaning "confirmed disease." It is said that He "*bare*" our sicknesses. The word rendered "bare" in the Greek means to take away or remove. The Authorized Version margin gives a cross reference to 2 Corinthians 5:21 ("*He hath made Him to be sin for us*") and 1 Peter 2:24 ("*His own self bare our sins in His own body on the tree*") and Isaiah 53:4, showing that the translators of the Bible into English clearly connected this passage with the substitutionary work of Christ at Calvary—and that it means more than the fact that Christ as a Man of Sorrows *sympathized* with all in sickness and suffering.

It also appears from the words quoted by Matthew that the Lord did His healing work on the *ground of His forthcoming substitutionary death on the cross,* for we must not forget that the sacrifice on Calvary is *timeless* in its scope. It reached back to the ages preceding it even as it reaches forward into the ages of ages yet to come. Therefore in one respect, deliverance from sickness is part of the "gospel." But in another, *it does not mean that knowledge of this is essential to salvation.*

There are many in bondage here, because eager souls urge upon them that Christ "bare our sicknesses" on the cross, and therefore their "salvation" is incomplete if they cannot turn away from "means" and trust Him with their bodies as implicitly as they did with their souls. Let us take care that none put a stumbling block in another's way by pressing upon others the stage of faith they may have been brought to themselves. It is here that the danger of "soul-force" comes in! Let us bear witness of all that we have proved of the grace of

God, but at the same time leave to the Holy Spirit His work of co-witnessing to those He is leading on—always as they are able to bear it.

The substitutionary work of Christ on the cross was a FULL REDEMPTION. It would not have been so had He *not* dealt with our sicknesses as well as our sins—our infirmities and *all that has come to us through our first birth into the old Adam race.* But this redemption, *complete in Christ,* can only be apprehended by each one little by little under the teaching of the Holy Spirit. "Let us therefore not judge one another any more: but judge this rather, that no man put a *stumbling block* . . . in his brother's way" (Romans 14:13)—that is, the stumbling block of forcing upon others our "experiences" as to the use of "means" or "no means," instead of encouraging them to rely upon the Spirit of God to reveal His will to each one individually. For we must *not* limit the working of God to our *personal* experience of His "ways."*

---

*Our space will not allow fuller reference to other aspects of this subject, excepting to say that there is much self-deception along this line; e.g., a child of God says she "trusts God" and does not use "means," but in some physical attack she retires to bed, and uses the best means of all (apart from the healing touch of God)—letting nature do her own healing work!

(2) HOW CHRIST TOOK OUR INFIRMITIES

"Who being in the form of God . . . made Himself of no reputation . . . and was made in the likeness of men" (Philippians 2:6–7).

The Lord Christ took our weaknesses, in the sense that He laid aside the glory of His Godhead and became man. He was, we are told, *in all points* tried as we are, *yet without sin* (Hebrews 4:15). His "weakness" as a *man* tried Him, but it never became a vehicle for sin as our "infirmities" often do. Witness His victory in the wilderness temptation. "If thou art the Son of God"—and therefore possessing by birth the divine nature and attributes—said Satan, "make these stones bread." And the Lord Christ could have done it! But He had taken the place of *man*—weak man—a "Son of *Man*" as well as Son of God. As a man His reliance must be upon God, His path one of obedience to His Father's will. He was "tried" and "tempted," although He was the Son of God. But He had taken our "weakness," and He must not fail in the path of being our Example if He would be our Substitute when He reached the place called Calvary.

(3) THE CROSS AND INFIRMITIES

"He was crucified through weakness, yet He liveth through the power of God. We also are weak with Him . . ." (2 Corinthians 13:4, R.V., mg.).

But where does the *cross* come in in relation to our infirmities? Listen to the words of Paul: "He was *crucified* through *weakness* . . ." (2 Corinthians 13:4). As the Representative Man, Christ hung as our Substitute on that cross. He not only bore our sins on the cross and carried us to the cross with Him, but the very cross was possible only because of His "weakness"— the weakness which He had taken on our behalf. He therefore carried to the cross in His own person our weakness and our "infirmities"—i.e., all that comes to us with our first Adam birth.

Here we see a deeper depth of the cross, reaching not only to our deliverance from the mastery of sin but to our physical weakness and "infirmities" of every kind. In Romans 6:6 Paul said, "Our old man was crucified *with* Him." Here he writes, "He was crucified through weakness . . . we are *weak with Him*." Our "infirmities" and weaknesses were dealt with on that cross so that they might become vehicles for the power of God to be manifested. This brings us to ask how this works out in practice. For the fact remains that these "infirmities" *are not removed* even though under some mighty manifestation of the power of God—intermittently, or continuously experienced in response to faith—they may *appear* to have become non-existent. For experiential light upon this paradox we must go to that wonderful twelfth chapter of 2 Corinthians and read the words of the Apostle Paul.

(4) PAUL'S ATTITUDE REGARDING INFIRMITIES

"Of myself I will not glory, but in mine infirmities [astheneia]*"* (2 Corinthians 12:5).

"In me first . . . for a pattern," wrote Paul to Timothy; and he is for us a striking object lesson, in many aspects, of the way the redemption of the Lord Christ on Calvary works out in all who will follow on in the path of the cross. Are "infirmities" which we take to Calvary removed? is the question, and Paul's experience answers "no." And yet it can also be said "yes" up to the degree in which they become enveloped in the power of Christ. Let us say again that the word "infirmity" means primarily "physical weaknesses" and what we

may call "character weaknesses," *not sins.* Romans 6 says distinctly that the mastery of *sin* is dealt with by the cross so that the believer is delivered from the power of sin. But the "character weaknesses" remain as the "bent" or "make" of the believer—which go to show his individuality.

But why does the apostle say that he will "glory" in them? Only because each point of weakness gives greater occasion for the manifestation of the power of God. Again and again he refers to his "weakness." "If I must needs boast, I will boast of my *weakness*" (2 Corinthians 11:30, Conybeare. See, too, 2 Corinthians 12:5–10). Was it not that his eyes had been opened to see a deeper depth in the cross of Calvary which maybe he had not known before? Is not 2 Corinthians 13:4 the key to 2 Corinthians 12:9? "My grace is sufficient," said the Lord, in answer to the apostle's third appeal that Satan's messenger might "depart from him." Was that grace manifested to Paul in the revelation of 2 Corinthians 13:4: "He died upon the cross through the weakness of the flesh . . . *I, too, share the weakness* . . ."? Yes, and through the death of

---

*It is important to remember that these "weaknesses" are all *because of the Fall* and the state of sin in which we are by nature born. All infirmities therefore need the blood of cleansing, even when not the vehicle of actual sin.

the cross I share too the life out of death—
"HE LIVETH through the power of God"—
whereby His strength shall become perfected in my weakness.

Now let us see how the adversary takes
advantage of our "weaknesses."

(5) INFIRMITIES AND THE POWERS OF DARKNESS

*"There was a woman which had a spirit
of infirmity . . ."* (Luke 13:11).

The record in Luke's Gospel of the
woman with a spirit of infirmity, placed
alongside of Matthew 8:17 and 2 Corinthians 13:4, shows why our infirmities must
be taken to the cross before the risen life
of the ascended Lord can tabernacle upon
them. This story of the bound woman reveals that *behind an "infirmity" can be the
grip of an evil spirit holding the victim in its
power.* A Greek scholar points out that the
word rendered "of" indicates the genitive
of origin, and the word spirit, "an evil de-
mon" or "evil spirit being." This case shows
how *any "infirmity" can be the ground on
which evil spirits can work*, just as behind
every sin arising from the old nature can
be an evil spirit feeding or inflaming that
sin. For example, the jealousy that comes
from the unregenerate heart may have be-

hind it a *"spirit"* of jealousy.

In contrast to this case, we have Paul's experience recorded in 2 Corinthians 12. Paul knew the cross in its depths of power if any man ever did. Following the account of his *acceptance* of the non-removal of his "weaknesses" so that they might become vehicles for Christ's strength, we read in chapter 13 verse 4 that in the extremity of "weakness" and "infirmity," he turns to Calvary and sees the way of victory, through the cross. Let us ring out again his words, about the Christ of Calvary— "HE was crucified through weakness . . . HE lives through the power of God. . . ." "I am *weak with Him*," in the weakness of His death, and I also "LIVE with Him. . . ."

In brief, as we put the two records side by side—the woman with the "spirit" of infirmity and Paul with the "power of Christ" tabernacling upon his infirmities—we can see clearly that our "weaknesses," dispositional and physical, are open camping grounds for Satan *or* for God, and that the *cross* with its message of identification shows how we are protected from the one and brought under the power of the other.

This is the crux of the whole matter. Our inherent weaknesses of disposition and character, as well as all the inherited weaknesses of the physical frame, are "camping grounds" for Satan or for God. "Spirits of infirmity" seek to hold every infirmity in their grasp, as well as every weakness of the body. How shall we escape their power? *Only by means of the cross.* "He was crucified through weakness." We are "weak with Him" on that cross, for He hung there in our place. Let us even in these things say, "I am crucified with Christ." Then as we abide hidden in the Christ of Calvary, we are out of the enemy's reach and power. *Through the cross* the risen life of Christ can envelop us, so that His strength is perfected in weakness.

(6) THE HOLY SPIRIT AND OUR WEAKNESSES

"The Spirit also helpeth our infirmities . . . for we know not . . . as we ought . . ." (Romans 8:26).

Here "infirmities" are described as *lack of knowledge,* particularly in connection with prayer. "We know not what we should pray for as we ought, but the Spirit. . . ." The Holy Spirit with compassion for the weakness and ignorance of the believer is given to "help" his "infirmity," especially in the way of overcoming ignorance. And in fulfillment of His office to reveal the Christ of God, He makes real the blessed fact that the ascended, glorified Lord is *touched* by the "feeling" of our weaknesses. He knows just exactly how we *feel!* Yes, His very sinlessness made more acute His "feelings" when He walked as man on earth. Is it not written that on the eve of Gethsemane, He "began to be sorrowful and very heavy," i.e., *distressed unto despair* (Matthew 26:37). Mark says He was "sore amazed," i.e., *under a panic of fear* (Mark 14:33). His spirit was sensitive to the faintest trace of unbelief and doubt and *criticism* in the minds of those around Him. He knew what was *in man* and so He did not commit Himself to man (John 2:24–25). He saw into the wrong motives of those who sought Him (John 6:26). He knew when His disciples were murmuring at His teaching (John 6:60–61), and was not taken by surprise at the betrayal by Judas (Luke 22:21) and the denial by Peter (see Luke 22:31), nor that *all* the disciples eventually forsook Him and fled.

Yes, He is touched as He watches His children doing these things again to one another. He knows what is *in man*—the cowardice and fear that bursts out in an Elijah, as if he had never stood on Mount Carmel and faced the priests of Baal; the boastful talk of a Peter which fails in the hour of testing. . . .

This brings us to the last point that

(7) OUR WEAKNESSES ARE A TEST OF OTHERS

"Ye know that because of an infirmity of the flesh I preached the gospel unto you the first time. And that which was a temptation to you in my flesh ye despised not . . ." (Galatians 4:13–14, R.V.).

These striking words were written to the Galatians by the apostle who had learned to "glory" in his infirmities. They show how *others* are "tested" by them and how they may be tempted to despise the earthen vessel bearing to them the messages of God, sometimes through infirmities which are visible. Deprecating comments about the messenger were current among the Corinthian Christians as much as in our day! "His letters, say they, are weighty and powerful; but his bodily presence is weak, and his speech contemptible" (2 Corinthians 10:10). It is thought, says Scofield in a footnote, that Paul's "thorn in the flesh" was chronic ophthalmia, inducing bodily weakness and a repulsive appearance! In any case, Paul said that through some "stake" in the flesh, Satan's messenger "buffeted" him! This shows how keenly the enemy takes advantage of our weaknesses. He knows how to direct his "buffeting" on the keenest point of weakness of our make-up.

Paul said about himself that it was directed toward his disposition to become "exalted above measure." Very few are free from this weakness—the weakness of being unable to keep steady under the using of God—or *the easing by Him of circumstantial trials.* Paul's "revelations" from God therefore had to be counterbalanced by some obvious "infirmity" which disposed others to "despise him," criticize his lack of oratory, and note his manifest lack of a "presence" which commanded the idolatry of the crowd.

And finally, the infirmities of *others* are a test of *our own* spiritual growth. If we are "strong in God," that strength should be manifested in our bearing the infirmities of the weak and not pleasing ourselves (Romans 15:1). "It is only imperfection that complains of imperfection," said one of the mystic writers. Our inability to bear with others' weakness only reveals our own.

May the Spirit of God open our eyes to see the cross in all its aspects, so that in all our "weaknesses" we may be a camping ground for the power of our living Lord.

GLEANINGS FROM THE
GREEK LEXICON

ASTHENEIA (noun): lack of strength, weakness; lack of energy.

Rendered *infirmity* in Matthew 8:17; Luke 5:15, 8:2, 13:11, 12; John 5:5; Romans 6:19; 2 Corinthians 11:30, 12:5, 9, 10; Galatians 4:13; 1 Timothy 5:23; Hebrews 4:15, 5:2, 7:28.

Rendered *sickness* in John 11:4.

Rendered *weakness* in 1 Corinthians 2:3, 15:43; 2 Corinthians 12:9, 13:4; Hebrews 11:34.

Note: Hebrews 4:15, 5:2, 7:28, and 11:34 include the idea of moral weakness.

ASTHENEO (verb): to lack strength; be infirm, weak, feeble.

Rendered *sick* in Matthew 25:36; Luke 7:10; John 4:46, 11:2, 3, 6; Acts 9:37; Philippians 2:26, 27; James 5:14.

NOSOS (noun): sickness, confirmed disease.

Rendered *sickness* in Matthew 4:23, 8:17, 9:35; Mark 3:15.

Rendered *infirmity* in Luke 7:21.

Rendered *disease* in Matthew 4:24; Mark 1:34; Luke 4:40, 6:17, 9:1; Acts 19:12.

FRESH LIGHT ON JAMES 5:14–15

KAMNO (verb): to be weary, faint as from

labor, faint or weary in mind, distressed with labor or anything else. *Used only in James 6:15* (as a participle): one whose strength gives way in consequence of excessive labor.

"Is anyone sick [*astheneo*, infirm, weak, feeble] among you? Let him call," etc., and "the prayer of faith shall save the exhausted one [*kamno*, faint or weary in mind or body]. . . . The operative supplication of a righteous man prevails much. . . ."

—(*Englishmen's Greek New Testament.*)

Note. A correspondent writes that the Greek word translated "prayer" in James 5:15 is rendered "vow" in the only two other occasions in which it is used, i.e., Acts 18:18 and 21:23. The word used for "prayer" in thirty-seven other passages is not found in James 5:15. "The *vow* of faith" seems to have been the apostle's meaning, therefore, as though the weary believer had been faltering and needed to reaffirm his surrender and faith in God.

CHAPTER 5

THE CROSS
AND OUR FACTIONS

OR

BE OF THE SAME MIND

L ET us turn to our Bibles, and from the
Revised Version read part of Philippians
2, beginning at verse 5: "Have this mind in
you, which was also in Christ Jesus: who,
being in the form of God, counted it not a
prize to be on an equality with God, but
emptied Himself. . . ." In the margin it
reads: "Who, being originally in the form
of God, counted not the being on an equality with God a thing to be grasped, but
emptied Himself, taking the form of a
bondservant, becoming in the likeness of
men; and being found in fashion as a man,
He humbled Himself, becoming obedient
unto death, yea, the death of the cross.
Wherefore also God highly exalted Him,
and gave unto Him the Name which is
above every name. . . ."

Note the words "Have this *mind in you*" which was . . . in Christ Jesus." Now read back two or three verses. "If there is . . . any *comfort* in Christ, if any *consolation* of love, if any *fellowship* of the Spirit, if any *tender mercies* and *compassions*, fulfill ye my joy, that ye be of the SAME MIND, having the same love, being of one accord, of ONE MIND; doing nothing through faction or through vainglory, but in LOWLINESS OF MIND each counting other better than himself; not looking each of you to his own things, but each of you also to the things of others."

Taking the words "Have this mind in you" as the central sentence, if you read back to the previous verses, or forward to the succeeding verses, you have a pattern of the mind which was in Christ. As you read forward, you are told how Christ being "equal with God," did not *grasp* at it, but came down from such a height and emptied Himself to become a servant—a bondservant, under bonds, bound to serve. As you read backward you are told of the (1) comfort, (2) consolation, (3) fellowship in the Spirit, (4) tender mercies and compassions, which are in Christ for the children of God; and filled with His Spirit they can thus be of the "same mind," having the "same love," of "one accord," doing nothing through faction, but in lowliness of mind esteeming others better than themselves. If every believer had thus "the mind of Christ," filled with tender mercies and compassions, how could they be anything but "of the same mind"? If all were of the "same mind" to *do nothing* through faction, how could there be "division" and disunion among the Lord's people? "*Do nothing through faction*," said the apostle, as he thought of those he referred to in chapter 1 verse 17, who were even "proclaiming Christ of faction," thinking to raise up affliction for Paul in his prison; and he himself shows the "mind of Christ" even as he writes, for he says that he rejoices that *Christ* is preached, even though not with purity of aim. He is not going to admit in himself "vainglory" or "faction" in response to their wrongdoing!

While Paul remembers the "faction," how he yearns for "one accord." "Fulfill my joy," he says to the Philippians. "Be of the *same* mind, of the *same* love." Christ is not divided. Then what causes division and disunion in doing the work of God? What is the reason that the Lord's children find it so difficult to be of the "same mind," and still more difficult to esteem others better than themselves? Those who are really joined to Christ as members of His Body—

who truly have Christ as their life—are certainly *one in heart*; they are certainly more or less of *one aim*—they want to please Christ. But they are so rarely of one mind. One in heart and in aim, yet not of the same mind! What is the cause of this? Do we see the importance of it? Do we realize so deeply the need of being of one accord that we can wait patiently for others with whom we are in co-service to come to the "same mind" before we take a certain course which may produce "division" or "faction"?

How the words strike home! *Doing nothing that you know will tend toward disunion in the Body of Christ.* Surely if we were all of one mind to follow Christ to Calvary, "becoming obedient unto death, even the death of the cross," there would be no "vainglory," no being "puffed up in the cause of one against another" (1 Corinthians 4:6, C.H.); but we would really possess "lowliness of mind"—the mind that brought the Lord Jesus from the place of equality with God, down to the position of a servant; the mind that caused Him not to *grasp* the throne—that made Him not to cling to being a "leader," but choose to be a servant. He was equal with God, yet He became a "servant"—a bondservant. If we were all of one mind to *serve* one another! If we all longed to be servants, and did not want to be "heads of movements," or leaders of work, or aught else, how quickly this lowliness of mind would unite God's children and make them to be of the "same mind" in the Lord.

THE SOURCE OF "FACTION"

Now at the back of all "faction" the great adversary is at work; he is the great divider, the Lord Jesus the great Uniter. What is the cause of all this lack of oneness of mind? Who produces all the division of mind among those who are one in heart? Is it not Satan the divider? Is it not he who assails the minds of the children of God, to prevent their having the "mind of Christ," and hence the "same mind in the Lord"? To trace the adversary's working in this respect we must first go to bedrock facts, so as to understand why the enemy can thus attack the minds of believers and cause division among the people of God.

Turn first to 2 Corinthians 4:4 and read, "The god of this world." Who is this? *Satan!* What does Paul say he has done? "The god of this world hath *blinded* the minds of the unbelieving." Has the devil power to blind a man's mind? We answer "Yes"—for so it is written, and his purpose is declared to be "that the light of the gospel of the glory of Christ . . . should not dawn upon them."

This is the bedrock fact which must be emphasized as lying at the bottom of all division of mind among God's people. The apostle declares that Satan—the god of this age—has blinded the mind of every unregenerate soul. Not only ignorant people in the slums, but professors in colleges and kings on their thrones. There is no distinction and no difference. The Bible declares facts as seen by God, and He says that all men have *blinded minds* until the light of the gospel shines in, and that this film or veil on the mind is placed there by Satan—the "god" or ruler of this world—to keep the truth—or light—out. All have needy hearts, but all have also blinded minds.

Now let us face the question: When a person receives the gift of eternal life and obtains assurance of salvation from the guilt and penalty of sin through the atoning sacrifice of Christ, does he *entirely lose the "film" or veil on the mind?* Or does it mean that at first he gets a "new heart," and loses just a little of the veil that the god of this world has put upon his mind? In brief: Is it possible for the *Christian* to have a partial "blind" on his mind? Let us repeat the question: Does he at once fully lose the "blinded mind," or does he lose the film just so far as he apprehends the gospel, and no more?—for truth (or light) alone disperses the veil on the minds of men, and the extent of the light which shines into the mind determines the extent of the liberation of the mind from the veil of Satan.

This basic fact is most important for you to apprehend—it is the key to all division among God's people. For it seems clear that it is possible to have a "new heart" and a new life without a *fully renewed mind*. It certainly is clear from the facts of life and the present condition of the true Church of Christ. The mind of the Christian can be full of all kinds of things, injected there by the god of this world; and these injected thoughts—"views," "ideas," "theories"—are the causes of division, for if the *mind* of every Christian were truly renewed, it seems simple logic to say that all believers would be of the "same mind"—having the mind of Christ.

Now turn to 2 Corinthians 11:3. The apostle writes to the Corinthian Christians, "I fear, lest by any means, as the serpent beguiled Eve in his craftiness, your *minds* should be corrupted. . . ." Paul knew that even as the god of this world had blinded the minds of the unbelieving, so he could attack the minds of God's children and beguile them. "The serpent beguiled Eve in his craftiness." It was not her heart but her *mind* which he first attacked, and it is not your hearts but your minds which he also attacks to lead you away from simple trust and "purity" toward Christ. Eve was fooled by the subtlety of the serpent. She was innocent, but became ensnared through her mind . . . admitting thoughts suggested by Satan and accompanied by his beguiling power which paralyzes the mind and keeps it from acting and *judging the issues of every action.* Yes, Satan can attack the minds of the Lord's children. Satan could weave his wiles to draw you on until you are ensnared, and then you would find you lose your power of will. You first let your mind be charmed and cease to reason; then you lose your power of will to resist; and then you are deceived.

The mind must not only have all the old "blind" of Satan taken off, but it must be renewed and then covered by the helmet of salvation. You may have "put away the old man" as "concerning your former manner of life" (Ephesians 4:22, R.V.) without also a definite transaction with God so that you become "renewed in the spirit of your mind" (Ephesians 4:23). You are transformed *only* "by the renewing of your mind" (Romans 12:2).

"REVELATIONS" THAT DIVIDE

When the mind is renewed, it must then be used. And I want to say to you in the strongest way I possibly can say it, DO NOT LET YOUR MIND "LIE FALLOW" and become "passive," for as you allow your mind to cease to think, and reason, and judge, and bring to the verdict of the Book all the departments of your life—your experience and your actions—you are inviting Satan's beguilings into your mind. So few Christians understand Satan's beguilings of the mind that he is able to give them distorted views of the things of God, and of themselves—and of their friends, their future, their circumstances, and even their needs—without their recognizing the source of these distortions! Satan can give you such curious visions that only the truth of the Word—the pure light of the gospel—can expose them. Many have been led off into strange "leadings" by following sudden suggestions to the mind, believing they were obeying God. Others believe they have "revelations" from God which are going to move the world, but the only outcome is faction and division in the Church!

Passivity of mind is the "ground" which is given by the believer for these beguilings of Satan. Many Christians who desire to be "led of the Spirit" seem to think that they are not to reason, and to weigh and judge every suggestion which appears to come from God in the light of the Word. They think to be "led of the Spirit" means to follow every impulse and suggestion given to the mind—especially if it comes when in prayer—and so they let their minds lie "passive" to receive these suggestions. The Lord said to the Jews, "Why even of yourselves judge ye not what is right?" (Luke 12:57). If you are to escape Satan's special beguilings of the mind at the present time, you must not let it lie fallow—unused. You must not let it drift, nor let yourself go into "visions of the future" and be dreaming over the wonderful things God means to do with you! Do not foster "visions" as to how God is going to use you! Oh, the breaking up of false visions and "vainglory" plans which God has had to do! How sad has been the history of many souls who *were* walking steadily and faithfully, and are now unusable by God—high and dry on the shore. It has all come in through Satan's beguiling of the *mind*—suggestions, ideas, distorted visions, curious conceptions of almost every spiritual truth; all ending in factions and divisions in the Church of Christ.

THE "MIND" THAT WAS IN CHRIST!

"Have this mind in you which was in Christ Jesus, who . . . counted it not a prize to be grasped, to be on an equality with God, but . . . humbled Himself, becoming obedient unto death, yea, the death of the cross." With all my heart and soul and strength I would put before you the path of the cross as the safe path today. I put before you the path of meek and lowly service following in the footsteps of the Lord. Turn away from all vainglorious visions of what you think you are to be in the Church of Christ, and be satisfied to be a servant! Let us be content to be the *servants* of God! See to it, children of God, that Satan does not beguile your mind from *simplicity*—the simplicity which is toward Christ in steady, faithful service to Him.

Then let us remember that Satan can do nothing with us *against our will.* You can choose to say, "I deliberately refuse every bit of ground in my mind to Satan's evil spirits [for it is by his evil spirits that he does his work]. I refuse to allow 'deceiving spirits' with 'teachings' from Satan to enter my mind and beguile it. I ask God to give me a new mind—the mind of Christ!" And that mind, remember, is to be an active one—that is, one in *full use* in everything you do.

"More evils are wrought for want of thought than want of heart," they say. It ought not to be said of the Lord's children. But with so many, their minds are not free to act in the liberty wherewith Christ has made us free. They act as if they had no "mind," and that is why they run around and ask everybody else what *they* think. They are trying to get the use of other people's minds and are thus swayed and tossed about by every wind of doctrine. Souls who have heard the truth at these conventions for years, have they not the discernment and knowledge to tell whether a thing is of God? They have been living on what Mr. So-and-so says. He says it, therefore it must be right. But we must bring all things to the test of the Book and prove all things if we are to be intelligent in the use of a renewed mind.

In asking another's opinion, we have also to remember that it is possible for a soul to be in communion with God—in fellowship with Him in the spirit—and yet to admit one suggestion of Satan to his mind which will mislead him and warp his judgment in many ways. It is therefore not safe to judge as "from God" anything that another says purely because his life and character bear marks of fellowship with God. It is not a question of his character but of his *mind*. If we are to accept as infallible truth all that is said to be from God *on the ground of the character and life of a worker*, it would remove the standard of truth from the written Word to the character of the teacher.

God does not cast His children off the moment they have admitted a distorted view of the truth into their minds. Rather, He patiently waits until the real truth dawns; which it surely will, sooner or later, if they are *honest* and with open minds seek to do the will of God with all their hearts (John 7:17).

Ask the Lord to liberate your mind to act freely. Ask Him to break away from it every thought injected by the enemy. It is possible for Satan to find an entrance to the mind by pretending to be God. He knows you would otherwise never open your mind to the suggestion or thought. Numbers of God's children have followed deceiving spirits because they have believed everything that came to their minds on their knees to be from God, and consequently they have become unreasonable, obstinate, and unyielding. Sometimes they have carried out plans to the ruin of their families and to the ruin of their Christian service, believing they were carrying out some plan revealed by God.

Take heed that you do not travesty the truth of surrender to God as meaning that your mind is to become a blank. I read in one paper of a Christian worker who said it took him six months to get his mind "empty" so that God could get control of his body. Well, when he thus gave up control, *the devil took it*, for God "controls" a man through his own volition in cooperation with the Holy Spirit. Refuse to let your mind be passive, to let yourself become a machine, for God seeks to give you a new mind which will intelligently enter into His purposes and apprehend His will. "Be renewed in the spirit of your mind," and "be not unwise, but *understanding* what the will of the Lord is" (Eph. 4:23, 5:17).

Lastly we read in 1 Peter 1:13, "Gird up the loins of your mind." Those who are kept in perfect peace are those whose minds are stayed on God (Isaiah 26:3). To "gird up the mind" means to use it every step of the way: to act and think as an intelligent human being accountable to God in all things—one whom God has recreated with a new heart and a new mind. Then, the Lord says, *"I will put My laws into their minds"* (Hebrews 8:10). Feed well on the written Word; fill your mind with it, so that you will not need to be running for your Bible to look up verses. God will put His laws—or will—into your minds, if you will do your part by reading His Word, and you will find His Spirit in-working it to your mind so that it becomes wrought into every thought. Then when you need light on your path, the Word will come to your mind in a moment.

I fear that, with many of us, our great idea of "power for service" means that the Lord will make things easy for us to do. We want power to do things easily, so as to avoid all difficulty and labor in our doing them. We want miraculous guidance to save us trouble. You go on your knees and pray and then get up and open your Bible. The first verse you see you act upon, apart from all intelligent use of the mind and judgment in weighing and considering what is right to do. And what absurd things people have done through thus acting upon some verse they have read "after praying"!

Then, too, because the Lord, in the central depth of your spirit, gave you a verse one day, for the rest of your life some of you fear to act without a "verse"! And once you have a "verse," there is no one who can move you from your purpose to act upon it.

Remember, what comes from God comes from the inner shrine where He dwells, deep down in your spirit; and what comes to you from *outside*, injected into your mind, most often comes from the "world rulers of this darkness." When your mind is full of His law—His written Word—you do not need any miraculous guidance to tell you not to steal. How is this? Because you know it is wrong. His Word—or His law—is in your mind. Thus God can write His thoughts upon your heart and in your mind until you know His will, because your Bible has become incorporated in you. If we were filled with the words of this Book, instead of being filled with other people's thoughts and ideas, we would know the mind of God.

It is possible for the mind of a child of God to have in it many things which ought to be removed: an unkind thought about another of God's children which makes a barrier; a prejudice against this one or that one without any reason. These are ideas which Satan has injected into the mind in years past, and the soul is not conscious that they are *coloring* the life. Let us ask the Lord to liberate our minds from bondage, from being compressed and narrow, selfish, small, and cramped.

In the liberated mind there must be no "ground" given to Satan's "fowls of the air," either to put something in or to take the truth out. The Lord Jesus says in the parable of the sower, as recorded by Matthew, that the "fowls of the air" snatch away the seed; and He adds that it is Satan who does this work. But Satan is not omnipresent. He works through myriads of evil spirits—described by our Lord as "fowls of the air," for they come and take away the seed. Let us refuse entry to them and give them no ground, relying upon the Holy Spirit to keep the will steady and true to God, putting on the "whole armor of God" that we may be able to "withstand them in the evil day, and having overthrown them all, to stand unshaken" (Ephesians 6:13, Conybeare).

CHAPTER 6

TWO ASPECTS OF THE CROSS

IT is because the children of God do not apprehend the two aspects of crucifixion with Christ that they fail to realize abundant life in practical experience. The objective finished work of Christ in His death and resurrection is the basis of the subjective work of the Holy Spirit in us.

Objectively, the death of Christ was not only a propitiation for sin but was, in the purpose of God, the death of all for whom He died. In our position before God we who are believers are *in* Him, the Cleft Rock— *planted* into His death. The Holy One became a curse for the accursed ones, that the accursed Adam-life might be nailed to the cross with the substitute, the Lamb of God.

Subjectively, it is the work of the Spirit of God to apply to us the power of Christ's death and resurrection, to bring us inwardly into correspondence with our "position" in Christ—crucified, buried, risen, and ascended in the Redeemer.

The "objective" and "subjective" aspects must both be made real to the soul by the power of the Holy Spirit if "life out of death" is to be known in practical reality.

On our part, if we have been brought by the mercy of God to truly hate ourselves—our "own life" (Luke 14:26) as well as our sins—and to recognize that all is accursed, being heartily willing to renounce all that we ourselves have, we may turn to Calvary and see that in Christ we are delivered, being dead to that wherein we were held (Romans 7:6).

In dependence upon the Divine Spirit, we may appropriate the death of Christ as our death and count upon the immediate inflow of the life of the risen Lord to possess us to the fullest capacity of the earthen vessel. From this point—the faith position that we *have been* crucified with Christ—we may expect the Holy Spirit to bear witness, and "make to die the doings of the body" in ever-deepening power.

The Eternal Spirit—charged with the work of applying *to* us the death and of communicating *through* us the resurrection life of Christ—will cause us always to bear about the dying of Jesus. Thus shall be manifested in our mortal flesh the very life of Jesus! And in the power of that endless life, we shall be energized to labor according to His working—working *in us mightily.*

Particulars of the magazine
The Overcomer
may be obtained from:

The Overcomer Literature Trust
9-11 Clothier Road
Brislington, Bristol
Avon, BS4 5RL
England

This book was produced by the Christian Literature Crusade. We hope it has been helpful to you in living the Christian life. CLC is a literature mission with ministry in over 50 countries worldwide. If you would like to know more about us, or are interested in opportunities to serve with a faith mission, we invite you to write to:

Christian Literature Crusade
P.O. Box 1449
Fort Washington, PA 19034